Answers Yo
Successful Pub

AUTHOR-AS-PUBLISHER

Cathy L. Davis

AUTHOR-AS-PUBLISHER FAQs
Answers You Need for a
Successful Publishing Experience
Cathy L Davis

Published by UpsiDaisy Press
Copyright ©2023 Cathy L. Davis
All rights reserved.

No part of this publication may be reproduced, stored in a retrieval system, or transmitted in any form or by any means, electronic, mechanical, photocopying, recording, scanning, or otherwise, except as permitted under Section 107 or 108 of the 1976 United States Copyright Act, without the prior written permission of the Publisher. Requests to the Publisher for permission should be addressed to Permissions Department, office@daviscreative.com.

Limit of Liability/Disclaimer of Warranty: While the publisher and author have used their best efforts in preparing this book, they make no representations or warranties with respect to the accuracy or completeness of the contents of this book and specifically disclaim any implied warranties of merchantability or fitness for a particular purpose. No warranty may be created or extended by sales representatives or written sales materials. The advice and strategies contained herein may not be suitable for your situation. You should consult with a professional where appropriate. Neither the publisher nor author shall be liable for any loss of profit or any other commercial damages, including but not limited to special, incidental, consequential, or other damages.

ISBN: 979-8-9863157-1-3   paperback
979-8-9863157-2-0   ebook

LCCN: 2023907659

ATTENTION CORPORATIONS, UNIVERSITIES, COLLEGES, AND PROFESSIONAL ORGANIZATIONS: Quantity discounts are available on bulk purchases of this book for educational, gift purposes, or as premiums for increasing magazine subscriptions or renewals. Special books or book excerpts can also be created to fit specific needs. For information, please contact office@daviscreative.com

DEDICATION

To all the independent thinkers and independent authors who blaze their own trail of success.

HOW TO USE

Questions are listed in chronological order, followed by topic if there are multiple questions for that category.

Table of Contents

What does "Author-as-Publisher" mean, and what are the benefits?. 6

How does making me the publisher help me as an author? 8

What do I write about — where do I start?. 10

I published my book a few years ago, but I'm not on Amazon. Should I be? 12

I have a blog I've been writing for 7 years …
    can I use any of that content for a book?. 14

Can I use images in my book?. 16

How can I avoid lawsuits when writing a memoir or nonfiction business book? . . . 20

How does all this new AI stuff and ChatGPT affect me as an author? 24

Do I really need a professional editor and proofreader? 28

How do I get testimonials or endorsements for my book?. 30

How do I figure out the price of my book? 32

What determines how well my book sells? 34

What is P.O.D. / Print-on-Demand (POD)?. 38

Can you help me get books printed but not through Amazon? 42

Why do I need to upload my book to both Amazon and Ingram? 44

When will my book be live online? 48

Somebody told me my hardback will sell more copies; is that true?. 50

How do I know when I sell a book, and how do I get paid? 54

What if I want my book translated into another language? 56

If I miss the fall holiday sales window, is there another time of year that is good for book sales? 60

What's the best way to market my book? 62

How do I create/organize a BOOK SIGNING event? 64

How do I sell my books at events? 68

What is an anthology?. 72

How can I contribute one chapter to an anthology?. 76

Why become an Anthology Sponsor? 80

AUTHOR-AS-PUBLISHER FAQs

What does "Author-as-Publisher" mean, and what are the benefits?

When you hire a team to help you produce and publish your book, it's much like working with a ghost-publisher. You bring your ideas, and they help:
- Develop your manuscript or edit and proofread one that you bring to them.
- Design your book cover and interiors.
- Facilitate a professional marketing and promotion experience.

Each of our authors is set up a as their own independent publisher, giving them the ability to:
- Minimize their investment.
- Maximize their return on royalties.
- Retain 100% of their profits.
- Retain 100% of their copyright.
- Access global distribution.
- Avoid self-publishing pitfalls.

AUTHOR-AS-PUBLISHER FAQs

How does making me the publisher help me as an author?

When you work with us, we make YOU the publisher.

That means YOU get ALL the ROYALTIES and AUTHOR COMPENSATION each time you make a sale, whether it's in person, online, in a brick-and-mortar bookstore, or from your own website.

- We teach you how to access your dashboard on both Amazon and IngramSpark (Ingram) to check sales and see when your next $$ deposit will be made.

- We teach you how to order your books at cost, resell for a profit, and ship directly to your buyer without you ever touching the book itself.

- You don't have to wait on your "publisher" to take their share of the royalty "pot" and MAYBE send you a portion of what really belongs to YOU.

- You get to avoid the lengthy process (18 months to three years) of searching for an agent to introduce you to a publisher, and having them make all the decisions for you.

AUTHOR-AS-PUBLISHER FAQs

What do I write about — where do I start?

AUTHOR-AS-PUBLISHER FAQs

When it comes to nonfiction, write about what you know, like, and FEEL.

Let's pretend you are a professional dog sitter.

Whether you are writing a blog, a social media post, or a draft of your book, make sure you are in sync with the answers to these three questions:

1. Who is your target audience? (EX: working professionals)

2. What do they wake up worrying about in the middle of the night? (EX: How can I make sure my dog is safe and happy while I'm at work?)

3. What's your RELIEF? What do YOU offer that solves this worry/problem? Offer them a SOLUTION. WRITE ABOUT THAT!

   NOW ... Tell me a story about how you helped a "dog family" feel better about leaving their dog with you while they go to work or on vacation. Storytelling engages your audience and invites them into your KNOW-LIKE-TRUST funnel. It helps them feel like you "get" them!

AUTHOR-AS-PUBLISHER FAQs

I published my book a few years ago, but I'm not on Amazon. Should I be?

- How are you using your book? If you use it for training and aren't concerned about retail sales, then NO. Amazon keeps most of your profit anyway. If you want to create one more place where people can find you, then YES. Having your book on Amazon is a big deal and helps your website SEO when your Amazon book link is on your website.

- Has your book been professionally produced (either by a traditional publisher or by a publishing vendor)? If so, then yes, you probably need to have your book listed on Amazon as well as distributed through Ingram.

- If your book is 100% DIY and looks like it was produced by someone who has never published a book before, then I'd avoid putting it anywhere, let alone Amazon. First impressions are everything, and you don't want to scare potential clients away.

- REMEMBER: You make more money when you sell your book from your website or at the back of a room when speaking. This pulls Amazon (or any other retailer) out of the mix so you don't have to share a percentage of your profits.

AUTHOR-AS-PUBLISHER FAQs

I have a blog I've been writing for 7 years ... can I use any of that content for a book?

YES! You absolutely CAN. We've helped several authors use existing content from their blog, organize it into sections, and create a book that ends up being an awesome marketing tool! INSTANT CREDIBILITY!

Content is KEY to establishing yourself as THE credible resource.

What if you don't have a blog? Be brave and start by making a list of topics you know a lot about. Once a week, sit down and write out 150 to 200 words. It doesn't have to be War and Peace ... keep it simple! Pretty soon, you'll have enough content to expand upon and use for a book!

AUTHOR-AS-PUBLISHER FAQs

Can I use images in my book?

AUTHOR-AS-PUBLISHER FAQs

Of course! Especially in nonfiction books, many of our authors include photos, charts, or illustrations in their books. The trick is to remember these things:

- If you did not take the photo, you must get permission to use it OR use royalty-free photos.
- NO, you cannot take a photo of something in someone else's book and reuse it in your book.
- Yes, you can use photos you have taken if they are high-resolution. High resolution means 300dpi or greater, in focus, AND larger than the final space they'll take up in your book.
- IF you hire a photographer to take photos for your book, make sure you negotiate who OWNS those photos — you or the photographer. You always want to own the photos, if possible. Depending on the photographer, they may let you own the photos and use as you want, while they retain portfolio rights. Many photographers will offer a Licensing Fee, where you pay them to use those photos under the conditions set by the photographer.

Continued on next page

- YES, you can hire an illustrator to draw pictures for your book. PLEASE talk with us BEFORE the illustrator begins so that you avoid re-do charges from the illustrator. They may also have a licensing agreement, although many of the illustrators we work with will let the author "buy" the right to use the images when and where they want as long as the illustrator is mentioned and can retain portfolio rights. REMEMBER: ASK UP FRONT!
- If all else fails, PLEASE ask us BEFORE YOU hire anyone to provide images for your book. It'll save you $$ and time in the long run.

AUTHOR-AS-PUBLISHER FAQs

"Working with such a positive and collaborative publishing team, was a wonderful experience! I felt supported every step of the process. The team answered all my questions and clarified any uncertainties I had!"

— Sharon Wible, Author,
The Left-Out Little o

AUTHOR-AS-PUBLISHER FAQs

How can I avoid lawsuits when writing a memoir or nonfiction business book?

Our policy is that we need to have an email from the person being mentioned that they have read the section where their name is used (even if it's only the first name), giving their permission to have their name used as written. It doesn't matter if it's a family member, former colleague from 20 years ago, or "first love" from kindergarten.

I'm amazed at how many people decline to have their name used in a book once they have read where/how their name is being used.

If the author cannot find the person or if they are deceased, then we recommend not using their name nor specific identifiers. You'll want to rewrite the passage so that NO ONE can figure out who it is that you are referring to.

We had an author (a medical doctor) who kept telling us that he had asked and gotten permission from his patient to use their name. I kept pushing for an email from both the doctor and the patient. I even had to threaten to not publish his book unless we had an email. Once he finally sent his patient a

Continued on next page

request with the section attached, the patient read it and DID NOT give their permission to use her name. We frantically, at the last minute, rewrote that section.

NOTE: If you have signed a legal document stating that you will not discuss "something" — EVER — you cannot turn around and write a book about it. Yes, we actually had an author think they could do this.

When in doubt ... ASK US before you publish.

"The Davis Creative Publishing team did all the heavy lifting when it came to the technical end of turning my stories into a real book. I will forever be grateful to them for handling all the ins and outs of what it takes to transform a dream into reality."

— Kim Carr, Author of
Dandelion, My House Chicken

AUTHOR-AS-PUBLISHER FAQs

How does all this new AI stuff and ChatGPT affect me as an author?

The AI industry changes on a daily basis. Literally.

We've been watching, learning, reading, and talking with industry pros, and here is how we are handling this topic ...

GOOD NEWS:
- AI is a great tool for inspiration or writer's block. It can research and write blogs, articles, and other content almost instantly. Please make sure you review every word and rewrite in your own words so it sounds like you — never just drop AI content into a blog (etc.) without reading it first.

- AI can assist with spelling, grammar, synonyms, and even generate entire pieces of text.

- AI makes writing more accessible to people who struggle with language, such as those learning a new language or those with certain disabilities.

Continued on next page

CONCERNS:

- I question the authenticity and originality of the work being produced. Some copy comes across with no emotion or depth.

- Some say the text generated is plagiarism-free. This appears to still be in debate, although I read where some sources are starting to embed invisible code to identify the source. NOTE: This also means it is currently not able to be copyrighted.

- AI can never replace human intelligence and creativity nor out-of-the-box thinking. It merely presents what is already out there in the "universe."

- You can read our AI Policy here: https://creativepublishingpartners.com/ai-policy/

AUTHOR-AS-PUBLISHER FAQs

> "Thank you everyone, for all of your help. It is impossible for me to believe that anyone can publish on their own."
>
> — Michael Yasny, Author,
> *So, You Want to Start Your Own Business: Everything You Ever Wanted to Know to Start, Grow, and Succeed in Your New Business*

AUTHOR-AS-PUBLISHER FAQs

Do I really need a professional editor and proofreader?

If you want to portray a professional brand, YES!!
- NO, your neighbor's cousin's college son who happens to be a literature major IS NOT a perfect resource. Editing school papers is NOT the same as editing a book.
- Your book is your primary marketing tool to fill your sales funnel.
- Why take a chance that readers will find mistakes in your content?
- Mistakes in your book infers you make mistakes in your business.

AUTHOR-AS-PUBLISHER FAQs

How do I get testimonials or endorsements for my book?

Every author needs a team of cheerleaders — people who have been there for you as you were researching and writing your book and are actively following you as you get ready to launch and publish your book.

How does this help YOU as an author?
- Invite several of your cheerleaders to pre-read your book and offer a genuine review of your book — sometimes called an endorsement or testimonial.

- Use these testimonials to increase your credibility and position you as an expert in your field.

- We add them in the front, inside of your book (before the title page) as well as using mini excerpts from 2-3 of your favorites on the back cover. A high-profile endorsement often gets used as what we call an "eyebrow" at the very top of the front cover. Keep these short and impactful.

- When you work with us, we discuss best practices and offer guidelines on what to say and what to ask for.

AUTHOR-AS-PUBLISHER FAQs

How do I figure out the price of my book?

We help you figure out how to price your book. Book prices are dependent upon page count. As we move into the layout process for the paperback, we'll have a better idea of exact page count.

We will provide you with a chart showing your book cost (wholesale price) through both Amazon and Ingram, including possible pricing (and profit) options you have for both the paperback and the hardback versions.

If you have signed up for an Amazon Best-Seller Campaign, your e-book will be priced at either $1.99 or $2.99 for your two-day launch. Once your launch is over, we'll want to keep your final retail e-book price between $2.99 and $9.99, which offers you a 70% publisher compensation (royalty) vs. 30% for pricing outside of those parameters. Quite often, the e-book retail price is around 50% (or less) of the paperback.

AUTHOR-AS-PUBLISHER FAQs

What determines how well my book sells?

Remember the acronym "VALUE." The price you charge for your book is dependent upon it's perceived VALUE, which can also affect how well it sells.

- V = VISUAL IMPRESSION. YES, you really can tell a book by its cover, number of pages inside, and its content. If your book is too thick, it WON'T sell as easily.

- A = ALIGNMENT. Make sure your message is in alignment with your content and makes sense to your audience. Consistency + Knowledge helps to establish "expert" status.

- L = LEVERAGE. Leverage your knowledge with your target audience. What do they wake up in the middle of the night worried about? Offer RELIEF for that in your subtitle.

Continued on next page

AUTHOR-AS-PUBLISHER FAQs

- U = USER-FRIENDLY. Use the "parts" of the book to your advantage. Studies show that eager readers follow this order for looking at a book: FRONT COVER + BACK COVER + Table of Contents = SOLD.
- E = EXPECTATIONS. Do your research. People who read books in your genre are likely to have other books like yours. Research what the competition is doing and make sure you offer MORE, NEW, or BETTER.

Be the expert you truly are and be willing to price your book accordingly. Then go buy that drive-thru coffee and celebrate your potential book sales.

"Working with you was one of the best decisions I made around getting my book published. Immediately after publishing my book, (you) invited me to join an anthology filled with other amazing authors and I was thrilled to be part of the amazing *Bright Spots* book. Not being a natural author, (you) made the entire process easy and understandable. I think I have become addicted to writing based on my experience with (you)!

— Connie Whitman, Author, *ESP-Easy Sales Process*, and Compiler of the *Ready, Connect, Grow* Anthology

AUTHOR-AS-PUBLISHER FAQs

What is P.O.D. / Print-on-Demand (POD)?

Historically, traditionally printed books were printed in large quantities at printing companies. You would need to buy books in large quantities to get better pricing and then store your "extras" in your garage or basement. Most often, you end up buying more books than you need and giving most of them away — especially if you happen to find a typo or necessary edit.

- Print-on-demand (POD) came onto the book industry scene in the early 1980s, after first appearing as color copiers and one-shirt screen printers.

- Ingram started POD for books in 2013 for Independent Publishers under the name of Lightning Source.

- Amazon followed shortly thereafter and began offering POD in 2015.

How does this help YOU as an author?
- You only have to buy the number of books that you know you can sell. We show you how to order your books at cost, and you have the freedom to order as few or as many as you want. Most orders ship within 7 to 10 days.

Continued on next page

AUTHOR-AS-PUBLISHER FAQs

- Buying your books "at cost" through Ingram or Amazon gives you pricing that is typically much lower than printing companies for smaller quantities. We help you determine your at-cost price and show you your retail pricing options, including your potential expected royalty per retail sale.

- When you need book quantities of 100 or more at one time, please contact our office, and we can help you find the best price through our vetted printing vendors.

- Accessing global distribution directly through Ingram gives you the same distribution as major publishers, giving your book greater access to retailers and libraries.

"Working with the people at CPP has been wonderful. They are professional, knowledgeable and very helpful. They are friendly, always available, and easy to talk to. I could not have accomplished this without them!

— Vicki Kinzie, Author,
Dreams That Drip Murder

AUTHOR-AS-PUBLISHER FAQs

Can you help me get books printed but not through Amazon?

Certainly! We work with a lot of speakers and trainers who want books to sell at events or to use in training but don't want them on Amazon. We work with an amazing list of vetted printing vendors and will get you the best pricing possible.

- Smaller, printed "pocket" books typically outsell e-books and audiobooks.
- Gain credibility and be seen as the expert you truly are.
- Avoid online sales and sell only through your website or in-person events.
- Our DynaMighty Mini Book is the perfect "calling card" for speakers, trainers, coaches, consultants, and sales professionals. https://bit.ly/DynaMightyMiniBooks
- A content powerhouse, it's smaller (4" x 6" or 5" x 8" or 6.5" x 6.5") and only 50 to 100 pages — making them easy to customize, quick to read, and most importantly, AFFORDABLE.

# Why do I need to upload my book to both Amazon and Ingram?

If you want your book available around the planet, you need to have your book uploaded to both Amazon and Ingram.

- Amazon is an online retailer, much like Target or Walmart. You can buy pretty much anything you want at any of these three retailers.

- Ingram, on the other hand, is a book publisher and distributor. All the major publishing houses, such as Penguin, Macmillan, John Wiley & Sons, etc., use Ingram (or one of its divisions) for their global book distribution. The Ingram global network includes over 40,000 distribution points around the planet.

- Amazon offers what they call "Expanded Distribution," which is actually Ingram distribution. We do not recommend that you buy Expanded Distribution from Amazon, as they are simply a reseller for Ingram and mark up the cost when they sell it to you. We DO recommend you set up your own account on Ingram and run your distribution directly through them.

Continued on next page

- Ingram took over library distribution from Baker & Taylor in 2019. So, if you want your book accessible to bookstores AND libraries, you need to distribute through Ingram.
- What this means for the Author-as-Publisher is that if you have a cousin in the UK, or perhaps Bora Bora, and they prefer to "buy local," they can walk into any of their neighborhood book shops and request your book. It does not mean your book will automatically be on the shelf, but it DOES mean the retailer can access Ingram Distribution through that store's computer and order your book.

> "Cathy, I love how you make a difference and save the planet. Books are for writing, repurposing, and recycling — nothing comes from nothing. You're awesome!
> — Amy Narishkin, PhD

AUTHOR-AS-PUBLISHER FAQs

When will my book be live online?

AUTHOR-AS-PUBLISHER FAQs

One of the great things about POD is how fast you can upload your book to Amazon and Ingram ... AND how fast your book is available for sale, not only on Amazon, but ANY Ingram online retailer, including Barnes & Noble, Target, Walmart, etc.

Whether it's your initial upload or a reload due to changes or edits ... that's the beauty of POD!

- E-books are typically the first to go live; digital files get checked more quickly.
- Paperbacks will go live next, usually within 24–48 hours of uploading.
- Hardbacks take the longest, usually a minimum of 7–10 days after uploading.

Keep in mind all of this is dependent on a few things not within our control:

- Busy seasons take longer (April, May, and October through December = peak).
- More books being uploaded at the same time causes all books to be delayed.
- Some retailers only update their online sites periodically (Barnes & Noble updates weekly).

AUTHOR-AS-PUBLISHER FAQs

Somebody told me my hardback will sell more copies; is that true?

Nope. You'll mostly sell more paperbacks, followed by audio books, then e-books. A recent study shows that even the millennials (younger crowd) are buying paperbacks in lieu of digital.

Hardbacks are somewhat trending right now ... more like a status symbol. Hardbacks are usually seen as "collector's editions" and sent to special people who you would like to "gift" a book as one of your supporters. It's nice to have it out there for the die-hard readers who ONLY read hardbacks, but it's not a big moneymaker. Hardbacks cost more money to make and, therefore, are more expensive.

Continued on next page

You have three options for the "look" of your hardback through Print-on-Demand (Ingram):
1. Casebound = same art as the paperback on slightly padded heavy board
2. Traditional hardback with dust jacket over a "linen-look" vinyl
3. Traditional hardback with dust jacket over the paperback/casebound OR a new custom casebound art (using a solid color is popular)

What do I put on the flaps of my hardback?
We recommend putting one or two testimonials on the left front flap (different than any on the back cover) and your bio (abbreviated) on the back flap with a new/different photo than you have previously used.

"Thank you truly for the masterful way you both worked your expertise and magic into my story. It is such a privilege to work with you and I'm so thrilled to be moving forward on design! Deep bow of gratitude to you all!"

— Julia (Harriett) Anderson, Author,
Under Construction: Healing Trauma While Building My Dream, and
The Woman Who Saved Love

How do I know when I sell a book, and how do I get paid?

If your book is on Amazon.com and available in bookstores and libraries through Ingram, you will automatically have your own dashboard on both of those websites.

We teach you how to access your dashboards, check sales, buy books at cost, and learn how much your next royalty check will be. You won't be able to see WHO bought your book or WHERE it was sold, but you WILL be notified of the amount of money they will be sending to your bank account.

An educated author is a happy author!

What if I want my book translated into another language?

Many of our books have been translated into Spanish, French, Italian, German ... and we have resources for many other languages. You'll want to start with a well-written English version, professionally edited and proofread. Once the English version has been laid out an approved, we then match you with a translator for the foreign language of your choice.

Additional foreign language questions and answers:

- If my book is originally in English and comes in as a #1 International Amazon Bestseller, how does that affect the Italian translation of the same book?

  Whatever level of Amazon Bestseller that the English version gets, it applies to all languages.

- Does my copyright cover all translation versions of my book?

  Yes, if you are in the United States, you have a U.S. copyright.

Continued on next page

- Can I use the same ISBN number on both my English and Italian translation book?

Each of your versions in a different language will have a different ISBN number. So, if you decide to do the book in Italian, and you have a paperback and e-book in Italian, then you'll need to use two more of your ISBNs. But ALL versions of the book can "ride the tide" of the Amazon Bestseller ranking based on the original English version.

AUTHOR-AS-PUBLISHER FAQs

> "Working with the team was a joy. We experienced a family emergency close to the deadline and the support I received from the editor was above and beyond. From the time I was asked to contribute until post-publication I knew what to expect every step of the way."
>
> — Mary Nunaley, Contributing Author, *Bright Spots*, and *Ready, Connect, Grow* Anthologies

AUTHOR-AS-PUBLISHER FAQs

If I miss the fall holiday sales window, is there another time of year that is good for book sales?

YES, there are certain times of the year when different types of books sell best.

The fall holiday sales season starts to jump exponentially in early November, peaking by mid-December. If you plan on taking advantage of this prime sales period, your book needs to be available to retailers no later than October.

If you miss this prime sales season, don't despair ... create your OWN season for sales. Once you identify your audience, look for additional holidays or local/national/global events/holidays/celebrations that you can tie in with.

EXAMPLES:
- Valentine's day / poetry / relationship solutions
- Mother's Day / Self-help and women's empowerment
- Hispanic Heritage Month / translate your existing book to Spanish

What's the best way to market my book?

"It's not about how well your book sells ... it's all about how well your book sells YOU."©

Think of your book as a cupcake. Book sales on Amazon are much like the sprinkles on a cupcake — Amazon gets the cupcake; YOU get the sprinkles.

The trick is to create opportunities to use your book as a marketing tool and to sell your book yourself.
- Create workshops, webinars, and training opportunities where you can include your book with registration.

- Make sure when you are invited to speak in front of an audience to either offer your book to every person registered (include the cost of book in the cost of attendance) and/or sell your book at the back of the room.

- Organize joint-venture promotions to reach new audiences with co-events. Example: If you are an attorney specializing in divorces, invite a financial services person who also specializes in divorces to do a joint event. You get exposed to their network and vice versa.

AUTHOR-AS-PUBLISHER FAQs

How do I create/organize a BOOK SIGNING event?

FIRST: Start local. Typically, local bookstores LOVE to highlight local authors. But don't stop there ... even the major chains like Barnes & Noble welcome local authors.

Adding these things to your to-do list will increase your chances of being invited to have a book event:

- Make sure your copyright page has been professionally designed and includes all the traditional info bookstores expect it to have (we do that for you!).

- Make sure your book has been set up correctly for distribution through Ingram. Local bookstores see Amazon as a competitor and will not order books from Amazon because they'll lose money.

- Stop by the store and ask for the manager. Have a copy of your book with you.

- Offer to do the marketing for the event through your social media and e-newsletters.

Continued on next page

- Hire a designer to help you design flyers and a tabletop sign, both of which can be printed at your local printshop or online resource.

Your local retailer will be thrilled to have you promote your event at their store!

> "Davis Creative Publishing aided me in creating my G.R.I.T. series of anthologies breaking down the four aspects of G.R.I.T: GROWTH, RESILIENCE, INTENTION & TENACITY. Publishing these books with Cathy and her team transforms the lives of the contributing authors and readers alike — bringing hope & inspiration through stories of overcoming life's obstacles."
>
> — Jennifer Bardot, Founder, G.R.I.T. Community

AUTHOR-AS-PUBLISHER FAQs

How do I sell my books at events?

As a professional speaker, having your book onsite at an event creates the opportunity to get your book in the hands of the event attendees, whether you are giving it away or selling at the back of the room.

One of the great things about Print-on-Demand and event planning, is that you have:
- Greater control over your Author-As Publisher pricing.
- The freedom to order only the number of books you need.
- The ability to order and ship directly to your event location.

When selling your book at events, you'll want to first:
- Gain permission from the event planner to sell on-site.
- Invite a trusted "table team" to be at your back-of-the-room table to take money and answer questions.
- Have an 18" x 24" (or similar) sign made to sit on your table. Make sure it has your photo as well as the cover of the book.

Continued on next page

- Offer pre-signed copies as well as "bundle" with e-books and audiobooks, etc., or other books you have written.
- Establish a way to accept on-site credit cards such as Square, PayPal, Shopify, QuickBooks, etc.
- Ship unsold books back home. Never carry a suitcase of books with you on the plane. If you do it once, you'll never do it again (personal experience!).

"I was honored to be included with many other women who seek to help women become empowered. Through the guidance of Cathy and her staff, I got feedback that was helpful and encouraging. I loved the process and enjoyed meeting many other great authors who shared their stories to help others."

— Derlene Hirtz, Contributing Author in *Fearless and Fabulous*, and *G.R.I.T.: Resilience* Anthologies

AUTHOR-AS-PUBLISHER FAQs

What is an anthology?

An anthology is a collection of essays written by different authors, brought together in one book; it's also known as a "Collaborative Book."

You can either contribute a single chapter to an anthology that is already in process or publish your own anthology as a Curator/Sponsor, where you invite various authors to contribute chapters on a particular theme.

This gives you the chance to be a published author — without the financial expense or time involved in writing an entire book on your own.

The word ANTHOLOGY entered the English language in the 17th century from the Greek word ANTHOLOGIC, meaning "a collection of blossoms!" Our CATCH YOUR DREAMS Anthology Program allows you to tip-toe into the publishing world and blossom as a contributing author.

Continued on next page

When each author shares and promotes the book to their own audiences, you get exposure to new readers. Through this process of collaboration, more people learn about you and your unique offerings at a greatly reduced price.

We always have several anthologies in process at any given time, and many of those sponsors would be happy to include you as one of their contributors if your chapter fits their theme. Chapter length typically runs between 1,500 and 2,000 words. You will be assigned a Writing Coach to help you craft your chapter, and you even get to include a short bio at the end as well as your contact information.

"Anthology books are a true form of Collaboration. You and other authors write your stories, promote your book which gives you exposure to all the other author's contacts as well as yours. It is a true win-win-win situation for everyone — the readers, the writers, and the publisher."

— Joanne Weiland, Contributing Author in *Bright Spots*, *Engaging Experts*, and *Clarity Out of Chaos* Anthologies

AUTHOR-AS-PUBLISHER FAQs

How can I contribute one chapter to an anthology?

AUTHOR-AS-PUBLISHER FAQs

Many authors will tip-toe into publishing by writing a single, 1500-word chapter in an anthology. If you are already a published author, you may want to consider being an Anthology Sponsor and invite others to join you.

Biggest reasons to write a chapter in an anthology:
Over 1,000 authors have gone through our anthology program, and they all jump in for their own personal reasons, falling into at least one of the following categories:
- CONFIDENCE! Working with one of our professional Writing Coaches is much like getting to write your chapter while talking with your best friend and your therapist at the same time! Each of our Writing Coaches has a journalism/communications background as well as additional training as a therapist, life coach, or social worker. Many of our authors process through some very strong feelings as they decide to share their stories for others to read. Our Writing Coaches are there to help you open the gates to your soul to let the old stories out ... and in doing so, allow you to let in all kinds of new, wonderful experiences!

Continued on next page

- CREDIBILITY! Gain that expert status you eagerly seek. Each of our anthologies goes through the Amazon Best-Seller Campaign, and you are guaranteed to be able to add "Best-Selling Author" to your list of credentials!
- CONNECTIONS! You get to meet 40 co-authors who get to know you and your business ... and could be potential clients! Those same co-authors ALSO become referral partners with the potential to introduce you to people they know (most people have 1,000–2,500 connections just through social media).
- COST! Save money as a contributing author. Your cost to submit one chapter is typically 1/10th the cost of publishing your own solo book with a best-seller campaign.

> "(Cathy) created the Anthology Series business model as means of promoting and supporting women business owners around the world. (Her) expertise allowed us to bring our book, *The Anatomy of Accomplishment* from concept to the bookshelf. (Her) leadership allows women everywhere an opportunity to participate in the empowering world of entrepreneurship."
>
> — Erin Joy, Compiler, *The Anatomy of Accomplishment* Anthology

AUTHOR-AS-PUBLISHER FAQs

Why become an Anthology Sponsor?

When you become a Curator/Sponsor of your own anthology, we set you up as your own publisher and you get to invite the other contributing authors. The best part is that everyone shares in the cost of publishing and promoting the book.

As a sponsor, you get to establish the theme, the title, and the guest list. You also write the introduction to the book and your own chapter, and the rest of the book is written by the other authors.

We'll organize all the details — from contracts and invoicing to introducing your authors to their writing coach, setting up online meet n' greets, overseeing the timeline, and handling book orders.

You'll get to:
- Designate your own price points for author participation or build the anthology into one of your existing program offerings as an incentive.
- Use your anthology as an additional stream of income for your business.

Continued on next page

- Develop greater visibility for your business and solidify your professional image in the entrepreneurial community.
- Inspire and motivate women- and minority-owned businesses with your sponsorship, helping them to expand their brand and grow their business.
- Boost EVERYONE'S confidence, credibility, and connections when everyone becomes an Amazon Best-Selling Author!

GET ANSWERS TO YOUR PUBLISHING QUESTIONS

ask CATHY?

Have more questions?

Click the QR code to visit our "Ask Cathy" website page and ASK away!

We'll give you an honest answer in one of our weekly YouTube videos and/or connect with you via email to see if you'd like to schedule a phone call to discuss.

CATHY DAVIS

Books are in Cathy's DNA and have always played a big role in her life. Cathy Davis believes we all have a story to tell, and it is through sharing our stories that we can make a difference in the lives of others. Wisdom not shared is wisdom lost forever.

Cathy founded Davis Creative, LLC in January of 2004 after spending the bulk of her corporate career as a Designer and Creative Director for a global wealth management institution. Publishing their first book for a client in 2005, Davis Creative Publishing Partners is now a sought-after publishing industry leader, working with speakers, leaders, healers, coaches, and consultants to publish books that share their wisdom, inspire more people, and make a difference in the world.

With clients around the corner and around the world, Cathy and her team have helped over 2000 authors become published, with over 600 authors having #1 International Best Sellers.

CATHY DAVIS
CEO/Creative Director, Davis Creative Publishing Partners
Creative Publishing Consultant, Designer, Imagineer
Multiple #1 Amazon International Bestselling Author
International Speaker/Trainer
NLP Mindset Mastery Practitioner

Made in the USA
Columbia, SC
31 March 2024